Dr Faust's Sea-Spiral Spirit

Dr Faust's Sea-Spiral Spirit
and other poems

Peter Redgrove

Routledge & Kegan Paul
London and Boston

First published 1972
by Routledge & Kegan Paul Ltd
Broadway House, 68–74 Carter Lane,
London EC4V 5EL and
9 Park Street, Boston, Mass. 02108, U.S.A.
Printed in Great Britain by
Unwin Brothers Limited
The Gresham Press, Old Woking, Surrey, England
A member of Staples Printing Group
© Peter Redgrove 1972

ISBN 0 7100 7270 8 (c)

ISBN 0 7100 7271 6 (p)

To Bill, Pete and Kate

Contents

Acknowledgments

Grateful acknowledgments are due to the following:

To the various magazines and anthologies in which certain of the poems first appeared, including: *Borestone Mountain Poetry Awards, British Poetry Since 1945*, the *Cornish Review, England Swings SF, The Frontier of Going, Holding Your Eight Hands, The Kingdom of Granite*, the *Listener, New Poems 1971, Oasis, Outposts, Oyster, Poetry and Audience, Poetry Book Society Christmas Supplement 1970*, the *Poetry Review, Poetry St Ives, Second Aeon, Ten Quiet Shouters*, the *Transatlantic Review, Vortex, Wave.*

To the several private presses, collaboration with which has been a great pleasure and instruction. These include: Poet and Printer Press, the Sceptre Press, the Sycamore Press, Second Aeon Press and Richard Gilbertson's Manuscript Series.

To the BBC's regular programme, 'Poetry Now', and to various other broadcast programmes in which certain poems also appeared.

To *Poetry* for permission to reprint 'Water-Witch, Wood-Witch, Wine-Witch'.

To the Beaford Centre for evoking 'The House of Taps' through their poster-poem project.

To the Arts Council for financial assistance which enabled the author to complete this book of poems and a companion novel, 'In the County of the Skin'.

Christiana

That day in the Interpreter's house, in one of his
    Significant Rooms,
There was naught but an ugly spider hanging by her
    hands on the wall,
And it was a spacious room, the best in all the house.
'Is there but one spider in all this spacious room?'
And then the water stood in my eyes
And I thought how like an ugly creature I looked
In what fine room soever I was,
And my heart crept like a spider.

And my heart crept like a spider into the centre of my web
And I sat bell-tongued there and my sound
Was the silvery look of my rounds and radii,
And I bent and sucked some blood, but I did it
With care and elegance like a crane unloading vessels;
I set myself on damask linen and I was lost to sight there,
And I hugged my legs astride it, wrapping the
    pearl-bunch round;
I skated on the water with legs of glass, and with
    candystriped legs
Ran through the dew like green racks of glass cannonball;
And I saw myself hanging with trustful hands
In any room in every house, hanging on by faith
Like wolfhounds that were dwarfs, or stout shaggy oats,
And I wept to have found so much of myself ugly
In the trustful beasts that are jewel-eyed and full of clean
    machinery,
And thought that many a spacious heart was ugly
And empty without its tip-toe surprise of spiders
Running like cracks in the universe of a smooth white
    ceiling,
And how a seamless heart is like a stone.

Christiana

And the Interpreter saw
The stillness of the water standing in her eyes,
And said,
Now you must work on Beelzebub's black flies for Me.

For Barbara

Minerals of Cornwall, Stones of Cornwall

A case of samples

Splinters of information, stones of information,
Drab stones in a drab box, specimens of a distant place,
Granite, galena, talc, lava, kaolin, quartz,
Landscape in a box, under the dull sky of Leeds—
One morning was awake, in Cornwall, by the estuary,
In the tangy pearl-light, tangy tin-light,
And the stones were awake, these ounce-chips,
Had begun to think, in the place they came out of.

Tissues of the earth, in their proper place,
Quartz tinged with the rose, the deep quick,
Scrap of tissue of the slow heart of the earth,
Throbbing the light I look at it with,
Pumps slowly, most slowly, the deep organ of the earth;
And galena too, snow-silvery, its chipped sample
Shines like sun on peaks, it plays and thinks with the
    mineral light,
It sends back its good conclusions, it is exposed,
It sends back the light silked and silvered,
And talc, and kaolin, why they are purged, laundered,
As I see the white sand of some seamless beaches here
Is laundered and purged like the whole world's mud
Quite cleansed to its very crystal; talc a white matt,
Kaolin, the white wife of Cornwall
Glistening with inclusions, clearly its conclusions
Considered and laid down, the stone-look
Of its thoughts and opinions of flowers
And turf riding and seeding above it in the wind,
Thoughts gathered for millennia as they blossomed in
    millions
Above its then kaolin-station within the moor,
The place of foaming white streams and smoking
    blanched mountains.
Asbestos had found this bright morning
Its linear plan of fibres, its simple style,
Lay there, declaring, like the others;
Granite, the great rock, the rock of rocks,
At home now, flecked green, heavily contented in its box,

Minerals of Cornwall, Stones of Cornwall

Riding with me high above its general body,
The great massif, while its fellows, the hills of it
Rise high around us; nor was lava silent
Now it remembered by glistening in this light
Boiling, and was swart with great content

Having seen God walking over the burning marl, having
    seen
A Someone thrusting his finger into the mountainside
To make it boil—here is the issue of this divine intrusion,
I am the issue of this divine intrusion,
My heart beats deep and fast, my teeth
Glisten over the swiftness of my breath,
My thoughts hurry like lightning, my voice
Is a squeak buried among the rending of mountains,
I am a mist passing through the crevices of these great
    seniors
Enclosed by me in a box, now free of the light, conversing
Of all the issue this homecoming has awakened in the
    stone mind
The mines like frozen bolts of black lightning deep in the
    land
Saying, and the edge of their imaginings cuts across my
    mind:
We are where we were taken from, and so we show
    ourselves
Ringing with changes and calls of fellowship
That call to us ton to ounce across Cornish valleys.

The valleys throng with the ghosts of stone so I may
    scarcely pass,
Their loving might crush, they cry out at their clumsiness,
Move away, death-dealing hardnesses, in love.
The house is full of a sound of running water,'
The night is a black honey, crystals wink at the brim,
A wind blows through the clock, the black mud outside
Lies curled up in haunches like a sleeping cat.

Shadow-Silk

Rapid brothy whispers in the bed.
It was like silk splitting in me.
The house is full of the sound of running water.
A wind blows through the clock.
It is like a frail leaf-skeleton
Shivering in a casket.
We are heels over ears in love.
The window-frame blackens.
Below, the trees flood darkly,
The wind butts in the curtain
A doddering forehead.
We have a one candle.
Your hair is like a weir,
Or fields of posture,
In terrace upon terrace
Rising forest murmur,
And across the garden
Frothily flows the ghost.
The night is black honey,
Presses hard on the glass.
A sudden set! The stars are out.
This is too much; adventuring nectars
Wink with packed crystals
That hang depth upon depth
Age clotting the frame.
I must close this picture-book.
I must wade through these shadows.
Black springs from the corners
Brim the quartz-crystals
Engorge the ewers
Flood from the cupboards
Soaking the dresses
Pile under the bed
In black satin cushions.
That candle is unsnuffable!
We are afloat!
But the ring on your finger
Spins without stirring,

Shadow-Silk

I pad through the undertow
Reach out and close
That heavenly almanac.
Our wonder still lingers
Over the covers
As within the pages
All the stars glitter.
A wind blows through the clock
And across the garden
Frothily flows the ghost.

The Moon Disposes

Perranporth beach

The mountainous sand-dunes with their gulls
Are all the same wind's moveables,
The wind's legs climb, recline,
Sit up gigantic, we wade
Such slithering pockets our legs are half the size,
There is an entrance pinched, a plain laid out,
An overshadowing of pleated forts.
We cannot see the sea, the sea-wind stings with sand,
We cannot see the moon that swims the wind,
The setting wave that started on the wind, pulls back.

Another slithering rim, we tumble whirling
A flying step to bed, better than harmless,
Here is someone's hoofprint on her hills
A broken ring with sheltering sides
She printed in the sand. A broken ring. We peer from play.

Hours late we walk among the strewn dead
Of this tide's sacrifice. There are strangled mussels:
The moon pulls back the lid, the wind unhinges them,
They choke on fans, they are bunched blue, black band.
The dead are beautiful, and give us life.
The setting wave recoils
In flocculence of blood-in-crystal,
It is medusa parched to hoofprints, broken bands,
Which are beautiful, and give us life.
The moon has stranded and the moon's air strangled
And the beauty of her dead dunes sent us up there
Which gave us life. Out at sea
Waves flee up the face of a far sea-rock, it is a pure white
    door
Flashing in the cliff-face opposite,
Great door, opening, closing, rumbling open, moonlike
Flying open on its close.

Intimate Supper

He switched on the electric light and laughed,
He let light shine in the firmament of his ceiling,
He saw the great light shine around and it was good,
The great light that rilled through its crystalline
    pendentives,
And marvelled at its round collection in a cheval glass,
And twirled the scattered crystal rays in his champagne
    glass.
He spun the great winds through his new hoover
And let light be in the kitchen and that was good too
For he raised up the lid of the stock-pot
And dipped a deep spoon in the savours that were rich
And swarming, and felt the flavours live in his mouth
Astream with waters. He danced to the fire and raked it
    and created red heat
And skipped to the bathroom and spun the shining taps
Dividing air from the deep, and the water, good creature,
Gave clouds to his firmament for he had raked the bowels
Of the seamy coal that came from the deep earth.
And he created him Leviathan and wallowed there,
Rose, and made his own image in the steamy mirrors
Having brooded over them, wiping them free
Again from steamy chaos and the mist that rose from the
    deep,
But the good sight faded
For there was no help, no help meet for him at all,
And he set his table with two stars pointed on wax
And with many stars in the cutlery and clear crystal
And he set thereon fruits of the earth, and thin clean
    bowls
For the clear waters of the creatures of earth that love to
    be cooked,
And until the time came that he had appointed
Walked in his garden in the cool of the evening, waited.

The Curiosity-Shop

It was a Borgia-pot, he told me,
A baby had been distilled alive into the pottery,
He recommended the cream, it would make a mess of
    anybody's face;
My grief moved down my cheeks in a slow mass like
    ointment.

Or there was this undine-vase, if you shook it
The spirit made a silvery tinkling inside;
Flat on the table, it slid so that it pointed always towards
    the sea.
A useful compass, he said.
I could never unseal this jar, tears would never stop
    flowing towards the sea.

Impatiently he offered me the final item, a ghoul-sack,
I was to feed it with rats daily unless I had a great enemy
Could be persuaded to put his head inside;
That's the one! I said,
That's the sackcloth suit sewn for the likes of me
With my one love's grief, and my appetite for curiosity.

Young Women with the Hair of Witches and no Modesty

'I loved Ophelia!'

I have always loved water, and praised it.
I have often wished water would hold still.
Changes and glints bemuse a man terribly:
There is champagne and glimmer of mists;
Torrents, the distaffs of themselves, exalted, confused;
And snow splintering silently, skilfully, indifferently.
I have often wished water would hold still.
Now it does so, or ripples so, skilfully
In cross and doublecross, surcross and countercross.
A person lives in the darkness of it, watching gravely;

I used to see her straight and cool, considering the pond,
And as I approached she would turn gracefully
In her hair, its waves betraying her origin.
I told her that her thoughts issued in hair like
    consideration of water,
And if she laughed, that they would rain like spasms of
    weeping,
Or if she wept, then solemnly they held still,
And in the rain, the perfumes of it, and the blowing of it,
Confused, like hosts of people all shouting.
In such a world the bride walks through dressed as a
    waterfall,
And ripe grapes fall and splash smooth snow with jagged
    purple,
Young girls grow brown as acorns in their rainy climb
    towards oakhood,
And brown moths settle low down among ivories wet
    with love.
But she loosened her hair in a sudden tangle of
    contradictions,
In cross and doublecross, surcross and countercross,
And I was a shadow in the twilight of her late displeasure
I asked water to stand still, now nothing else holds.

Water-Witch, Wood-Witch, Wine-Witch

And when she came out it was raining, the night itself
Wanted to touch her, a silver stillness
Stood waiting, she was wet all through
Like a willow in the garden, wet apron
Shivering on an abyss. 'What is death,'
She quipped, 'but a lack of talent?' and spat at the
    rosebud,
'You are but breathing dust, and, look, you know
The language we call "Crossing the River", do you speak
The older tongue called "Wallow"?—watch the fish!'
And then the swans
Stabbed that wriggling porridge with their beaks.
She stabbed the oak once. It tore like grating silk.

She uncaps jars of venomous honey. I take her by the
    hips
And lift her down as from a tree. In the cornfield we make
    our love
And as we finish the air is thickly grassed with rain.
    Who was it
Who smelt even as she frowned in anger
Of blueberries and honey, in whose honour
Corn-lightning played over the horizon?

And if she herself grew old, the rain did not,
The terror of it and the mortal gaiety,
The kisses soft and money-cold, and there was
A squeamish clarity in every part of him. Blue denim
Singed with the seaspray, and the swim in the estuary
Not for the swim alone, but for the pang
Of their longer meeting, and for the wake that closed.
The tide oozed
And left a more earthly glistening, she was at first
Everything that fills you slowly, but after,
A moment longer than another's death.

She stabbed the oak once, and our hours
Cringed in the sunshine, the evening shadows

Water-Witch, Wood-Witch, Wine-Witch

Pastured gravely in the stabbed oak
Until at length the dawn made speech
Possible again. Then we woke
Among twining sunbeams full of breathing dust, gigantic
Upward nimble springs of growth and gold,
In spite of which she laughed
And gestured as if she were eternal,
And stabbed the oak once.

It was all coming together in wine or rain,
Much of it drinking, more leaving-taking
In wine-must, so that a fresh cigarette
Seemed the only clean thing left—wine encounters,
Creatures of lively blood and crystal
Left on the stabbed table like two glass shells
The wine-roar beaching in their sides
And the quarrel-knife between. She said
'Had you not been calling me,'
'Or you me,' he said,
'I'd not have come to you, or drunk,
Or laid in passion with the tide,'

'Nor I to you,' he cried.

The Passengers

He and she, on separate trains, speeding to meet

Among them all, those heads
In windowed rows like rows of bibles, testimony
bound
In skin and black hair, they seem the ones
Whose faces change, and their cigarette-smoke
Changes the same, as when a door to thoughts
Is shut or opened. Each one seems to think:

He: Why does the year turn round, and hand me ever
The same person? Now I can see
Every page in the book at once, she takes the book
And blows the print off, like a coarse black soot,
And the solid paper, thousand-walled white room,
Opens in banks of doors as she approaches.

She: Like our diaries lying wide open on empty pages
White with so many secrets we can't tell.

He: She turned to the window
Scarcely stirring in that dense silk dress
Filling her eyes with the moon deliberately
Brimming salt brooks buttoning the bright moon,
All dress and whiteness, nothing but the two,
Brilliant gaiety or white anguish.

She: A moth, enthroned, with gold eyes
And golden undershirt peeping from grey cloak
Had settled on the window where I turned
Blank from night with the moon full in my eyes to
look at him.

The Passengers

He: The clock moans, strikes, and strikes again,
The diaries lie wide open, filling me
With so many secrets I can't tell, the unread books
Lie like cold plates in greasy piles around me
For the banks of print
Were blown away at night-time, all we knew
Clumped far off into a crow of such tragic
    blackness
That when it settled on the branching stars
I wondered they didn't snap and fall.

She: I recall the deep hum of bees
Raising their eloquent temple, how the wind moved
With wings of black wheat, and all the stars beat
Like pulses of the one body, as we lay
Among the deep wheat, but I cannot remember
It seems so long ago
That start of beauty which in a moment
Seemed to destroy all ordinary speech.

He: Who was it that when I thought him coming
I could stop it, and make the night
Full of a smell of rotting stars, and my face
A dead man's, where decomposition
Starts with a look of sorrow?

She: We are passengers, swift-stitched across the
    country,
And as my train rushes into the tunnel
Winged seeds fly backwards. Who
Are we travelling to make, if anyone?

The Passengers

He :   Nothing but gaiety or white anguish. We had
        seemed parents
    Presiding over the work's birth, now once again
        we're lovers
    Hurrying to a meeting, hasty lovers, or dead ones,
        or
    Convalescent lovers—we! convalescents!
    As I drove out
    Into the raiding thunderstorm
    A great thing, like a lion's head,
    Lifted into the sky, and I was myself
    Merely a little slime containing angels.

She :   Blood has flowed, the danger's past,
    A tree is complicated when it's down,
    But now he rides into refreshed danger.

He :   With visible emotion once more in the trees
    I shall lie down again
    And travel once again so far my memory
    Will fail in love-spreadings.

She :   Will it rise this time on moss
    Heavy and green as soaked velvet sleeves, and
        flutter
    Like summer butterflies, or pump
    Like a great fat locust, and lose balance
    Like a fountain on itself for forgotten instants,
    None that we can tell? There are no sides
    And all is ritual, lover, we both ride
    These dancing cataracts of white. If the black
        blood
    Falls, the womb's blank and
    Danger's past and as the year turns
    It hands us ever the same person riding
    Into refreshed danger, not mine, not mine.

The Passengers

Both : Past these hundred bridges in their shaking stones
We rush against this blank wall
Like the great steam pile-cloud fretted with our
    speed
Hollowing away behind us, clearing. We follow
To dash against it, fountain
For a forgotten instant turned on and off and
    balanced
But springing in each season, followed.

A Small Death

My friend was gone. The sob wouldn't come.
They blow as they please. I owed her a sob.
It sank back into ashes. I tried again
It sank parching in vain. My friend was gone.
She wouldn't end. I couldn't begin.

I sealed my eyes shut. There photos awoke
Where she nodded and talked along a green walk,
Eloquent bee-hives, my rose pinned to her dress,
A shadowy face under a wide straw hat,
A sundial of sandstone warm with its time-telling.
The sob began, I fostered, obeyed it,
It reamed in my throat as she nodded and talked
Then turned under me gasping.

Seed brawled in my groin as she turned to me gasping;
My groin stung alight; the filament faded.
I woke from this stillness into a stillness,
Aching godseed of stars, a vase of black flowers, an
      empty armchair,
A night-laden window. I was emptied, quite emptied
Of a small distress. I looked down: one tear
Hung on a lash. It stretched to my cheek,
Snapped, sparkled and sank.
The sob wouldn't come. I owed her a sob.
My friend was gone. But she wouldn't end
I couldn't begin

The Youthful Scientist Remembers

After a day's clay my shoes drag like a snail's skirt
And hurt as much on gravel. You have mud on your
    jersey,
This pleases me, I cannot say why. Summer-yolk
Hangs heavy in the sky, ready to rupture in slow swirls,
Immense custard: like the curious wobbly heart
Struggling inside my pink shirt. Spring is pink,
    predominately,
And frothy, thriving, the glorious forgotten sound of
    healing,
And cheering, all shouting and cheering. With what
    inwardness
The shadows of autumn open, brown and mobile as
    cognac,
And the whole of my beer comes reeling up to me in one
    great amber rafter
Like a beam of the purest sun, well-aged; as it travels the
    grass
The dead smile an immense toothy underground, kindly.
I cannot explain why. You pointed out that the lily
Was somebody's red tail inside their white nightie
                So much so
That I am still sober and amazed at the starlight
    glittering in the mud,
I am amazed at the stars, and the greatest wonder of
    them all
Is that their black is as full as their white, the black
Impends with the white, packing between the white,
And under the hives of silence there are swarms of light,
And padded between black comb, struggling white.

I cannot explain this, with the black as full as the bright,
The mud as full as the sunlight. I had envisaged
Some library of chemistry and music
With lean lithe scores padding the long pine shelves,
Plumage of crystal vials clothing strong deal tables;
 had thought that the stars would only tug at me slightly,

The Youthful Scientist Remembers

Or sprinkle thin clear visions about me for study—
Instead you point at that flower, your dress fits like a
  clove.

The Idea of Entropy at Maenporth Beach

'C'est elle! Noire et pourtant lumineuse.'

A boggy wood as full of springs as trees.
Slowly she slipped into the muck.
It was a white dress, she said, and that was not right.
Leathery polished mud, that stank as it split.
It is a smooth white body, she said, and that is not right,
Not quite right; I'll have a smoother,
Slicker body, and my golden hair
Will sprinkle rich goodness everywhere.
So slowly she backed into the mud.

If it were a white dress, she said, with some little black,
Dressed with a little flaw, a smut, some swart
Twinge of ancestry, or if it were all black
Since I am white, but—it's my mistake.
So slowly she slunk, all pleated, into the muck.

The mud spatters with rich seed and ranging pollens.
Black darts up the pleats, black pleats
Lance along the white ones, and she stops
Swaying, cut in half. Is it right, she sobs
As the fat, juicy, incredibly tart muck rises
Round her throat and dims the diamond there?
It is right, so she stretches her white neck back
And takes a deep breath once and a one step back.
Some golden strands afloat pull after her.

The mud recoils, lies heavy, queasy, swart.
But then this soft blubber stirs, and quickly she comes up

The Idea of Entropy at Maenporth Beach

Dressed like a mound of lickerish earth,
Swiftly ascending in a streaming pat
That grows tall, smooths brimming hips, and steps out
On flowing pillars, darkly draped.
And then the blackness breaks open with blue eyes
Of this black Venus rising helmeted in night
Who as she glides grins brilliantly, and drops
Swatches superb as molasses on her path.

Who is that negress running on the beach
Laughing excitedly with teeth as white
As the white waves kneeling, dazzled, to the sands?
Clapping excitedly the black rooks rise,
Running delightedly in slapping rags
She sprinkles substance, and the small life flies!

She laughs aloud, and bares her teeth again, and cries:
Now that I am all black, and running in my richness
And knowing it a little, I have learnt
It is quite wrong to be all white always;
And knowing it a little, I shall take great care
To keep a little black about me somewhere.
A snotty nostril, a mourning nail will do.
Mud is a good dress, but not the best.
Ah, watch, she runs into the sea. She walks
In streaky white on dazzling sands that stretch
Like the whole world's pursy mud quite purged.
The black rooks coo like doves, new suns beam
From every droplet of the shattering waves,
From every crystal of the shattered rock.
Drenched in the mud, pure white rejoiced,
From this collision were new colours born,
And in their slithering passage to the sea
The shrugged-up riches of deep darkness sang.

To John Layard

The House of Taps

In the house of the Reverend Earth and Dr Waters
Moonlight strikes from the taps.
In the daytime, it is sunlight, full clear beams of it!
When they give water, these faucets, it is holy water,
Or river water, with green shadows of great ship-hulls
    gliding in it.
There are some also that bundle out exceptional ripe
    golden cornsheaves
And blackberries also, and pineapples and nightshade
    and innumerable other kinds of berries.
There is a large curved one like morning glory full of
    strong birdsong
And the smell of woodsmoke mixed with wet nettles.
Others I would not turn on again, not if you paid me, there
    are some
That throw out glittering lead, or rushes of fire,
And these are all made of wood, so that they smoke and
    scorch as they run,
And if they char too far they can never be turned off again.
There is another which is the faucet of pouring darkness,
    my eyes dim,
I grope, can I ever find it again to stop the darkness
    coming?
And there is yet another and this is the worst that seems
    to give out nothing
But when you look round there are certain articles
    missing.
But mostly they give out good things, sunshine and
    earth,
Or milk, or fine silky stuffs that glide out rustling,
The sleepy evening sounds of a town on the edge of the
    country
With rooks cawing as they settle, the clank of a pail, a
    snatch of radio music,
(Though I remember another that turned on a soft and
    continuous cursing
And from it extruded a pallid foul-mouthed person
Whose mouth foamed as I turned him off at the chest. . . .)

The House of Taps

But so many of them turn out good things, there is no
    majority
Of flowing blood or raw gobbets of flesh, it is mostly
Womansong, a stream of laughter or of salmon or bright
    blue pebbles—
And the lion-headed spigot that gushes mead and
    mead-hall laughter—
There are so many giving moonlight and in the day bright
    sunlight, rich dark barley-wine, and dew . . .
In this house of personages that prefer tenants to use
    the taps and sample the waters
And best of all to install faucets running with their own
    personal tastes and choices,
*In the great house of the Reverend Mrs Earth and Doctor
Waters*

                           To P.D.S.

The Wizard Gives Backword on his Deathbed

A choice dish nicely done; she whoops,
She swoops, she crams
The perfected goody into her great mouth
And without a gobbling word pops straight up to heaven.
I thank you, Sir. Are those quince, or mother o' pearl?
She smells of quince and her eyes are mother o' pearl,
And I hear bells and a kind of thickening footsteps
With a distant violin lie-playing, sweetly.
She is Mother of Pearl and offers nacreous cold,
The nights grow great and flicker through my eyes
And there she rides, stripped bare and wide awake
While from my teeth there's pouring such a cold
As holds me rigid in my bed, black ice, buzzing.
I've prepared enough black fly for her here, Sir.
It's choicely warm.
She sniffs, she lifts my gaudy lid a crack (which groans)
And snuffs out of my mouth the wonderful scented
    steam of pain.
Ah, Sir, would that there could at last be seen to shine
Some lightness, some brightness at my eyes, unborn, but
    shining there,
Like stars grown great with feelings, leaning over . . .
Or would that by their very own efforts, Sir,
These clumsy cries, these lolloping clouds of pain,
Could climb crooked and thinning as far as to where
Tumbling like thin glass from stillness
Light evolves our troubles, and solves them silently,
    Sire. . . .

Black wings I have made rush up, splash through the
    white ceiling.

The Wizard's New Meeting

I am startled by comparisons.
Ice melts from the thatches with the bare restraint
With which the flesh disquantities.
The sound of it beats back like small hearts in sheer
    spaces.
Stars lie in pools black as pupils
That return their stare, ice-irised. Though nearby
Fire thaws out the greenwood, slow explosion
Of smoke lifts through the chimney, here
My slow trudge snaps snow-crust and prints white darkly;
Blanched breath trudges across the night sky.
Things shiver and my breath is negatived;
In spread hand I hold the pane.

I slam the door. The brazier sucks
And glows in storeys.
I have the hair, the wax, a specimen of writing,
A pane of ice from the flooded churchyard.
I cast them in, they begin to wreck
And flicker with thin films, a gold stain spreads.
What do I think will happen, but steam and smoke?
I utter the words of vertigo, were I so strong
I should vomit as I spoke them, as some are said to,
Vomit as a thorough utterance. I am unsuitable,
But I will lend it blood.

The great book opens of its own accord,
Its snow-light floods the room, it comes, it comes,
The past has ripped away, there is a thin snow curling

The Wizard's New Meeting

And recurling over jagged mines
Of reserved lightning, I see boiling eyes
And a puckered mouth shouting silence so I razor,
The bowl fills and I grow colder
And the squalling bends to sip. I will not speak in terror
For looks of terror terrify the dead
To look so terrible, so I've studied calm,
Studied quietness till the right time comes
Which gives me calm. I am magic, then:

Magic enough to greet a person from the scraps and
        bones
Someone risen out of the feast of coals, a person
Fallen through our festering death, but risen up
And singing gladly of her current death.

A Taliessin Answer

What have you been?
A thunderharvest of twinkling grain.
A vivid gang of molten pig-iron.
The great man-eating skull that opens against the sky.
A whistle made from the wingbone of an eagle.

What have you been?
Escape from murder in the posthole.
A door opening on a stairway.
Frankensputin's monster.
The great luminous brain.

What have you been?
A nice meat pie without cartilage.
A wound in air.
The path of least resistance through the water.
The great Christmas reefer passed hand to hand along
    Hadrian's Wall.
The hiss of thick slices of bacon.

What have you been?
The loose shawl of a minister in the wood sitting alone
    on a log.
The subfusc overalls of a lawyer of note: much heated
    mud is flying.
A ladder of smoke on which a spirit climbs to heaven;
    I pass away.

What have you been?
A rain-begetter, a rain-splitter,
I had twenty-three aluminium eyes and long red hair like
    a horse's tail.
I was a frail sea-ear, a shell in the Atlantic fetch,
    listening;
An octagonal correspondence;
A leech daily regaled on the white rump of a lady of
    quality.

A Taliessin Answer

What have you been?
A pair of little old-fashioned spectacles,
A halo of inextinguishable guilt,
A brown violin on a white altar-stone,
A great vaulted godown, a baisodrome,
An undine-vase and a ghoul-sack,
A pair of enormous eunuchs playing draughts,
A cleft cathedral and a humiliation that suited me,
... and I have been foetal hair and an infinitesimal thumb
in a just mouth, a wispy cloud radiating a little above a
own full of children, and a bottle of ash with a green
velvet stopper; I have been a remunerated evil and a cold
tiger, a spayed gunman, a tiny clairvoyant power harmless
and green as a sunny meadow; I have been whirling
lights and spinning discs in a computer where lightning
and mineral submitted to supermarket interrogations;
I have been nearly lost in a pointed brush-stroke that
spread me carefully in lavish papery conversations and
debates among fishwives; and now the moon is filling
like a peepshow with things I have never been; I have
never been tendentious catastrophes, never newspapers,
a psychoanalyst, a pair of ill-matched lovers, not yet.

Which did you love?
When I had a small boy's notion of doing good, when I
     was
a mirror propped in a garden to repel toads and
     basilisks.

Tell Me, Doctor

'Dew on dead bodies: big joy'
Zolar's Dream Book) Doctor Solus

What do you make of the petals on the body, doctor?
She grew in the mirror at my back.
The dead body wet with dew made a humped shape
A wide-eyed body strewed with wet petals at the tree's
    foot
Like severed eyelids, so many eyelids
Shucked off and still we couldn't see. She grew
Old in the mirror, now I watch it empty over my back
And see only blank volumes, wide doors and staring
    ceilings
An unhealing blank place in the mirror,
And no she at my back. I was surprised at first
To feel my tears, until they grew like roots
Feeding to my mouth for nourishment, the salt taste
And the throbbing breakdown: I was surprised at first
To find my groin stir at the dead wet body
As if it wanted and began to seek out new life.
What do you make of the petals on the body,
Doctor? What of the dew wetting this dead body?
Should we not try to open our eyes under these
    showering
Dead things, doctor, as we shuck the old body off its
    back,
This blank place on the ground, as now we brush the
    petals off the face? Brush
The so many eyelids from the sightless face, doctor,
Brush scales off one pair of eyes at least.

29

The Flight of White Shadows

Over the crooked notice-board crying 'Private',
Over 'Greenlease' one half rented to the weeds
That munch its shivering windows, over the wide flat
    waters
Streaked by the gulls with long white cries,
Tripling the reed-hiss, killing the reflections,
The brusque shower comes. Each drop binds in itself
A terrestrial globe for nobody's inspection
Incurving sky full of meadow, gravid horse, farm, folk
    focused, each
Splashes itself many times over in leaves,
On rocks, worlds out of worlds, into worlds, before
    entering
The troubled horsetrough or the lying-down ditch
Still and long, that held a slightly vaster
Version of the sky. It is not a day for reflections,
Not even the smallest, of bird-bath, hoofprint, flowercup,
So slaughtered by swarming lives, the little bombs
Hacking away, whose twinkling self-assassinations
Tumble like consequences; confluences
Threading through tree-towers. A flap of thunder
Shakes out the clouds in the greatest of them all
Who, when in smooth vein, binds the sky into one salt,
One ferociously-curving whole whose theme is high sun
Boring his windy fire-holes—today is roof and ceiling,
Tiled and shattered snowing,
Racing acute edges on to the seashore.

Hordes strike, and forget themselves immediately, are
    gone
Water into water, or into stone speckling without
    sympathy,

The Flight of White Shadows

So what afterlife for the vehemence of sheer-fall,
The blackener of the sky with the limpid on earth,
Spater, bridge-bungler, gouger of fellow-water,
Bruised eggs streaming with a thin vision,
Smashed fruit under black banners? The same, though
Drawn through rock, honeycombs of knives,
Staircases of razors, chasms of scimitars,
Sandy scythe-galleries, division and redivision,
Unlikely rejoinings, green amnesias—all
To the one reflection down river-paths,
Passed down by the rivers, down to that larger,
To the vastation, which is not
The same artist for an instant either.

The Haunted Armchair

'... and hid his lord's money ...' (Matthew 25)

I want it not it not to go wrong. I want nothing to go
    wrong.
I shall guard and hedge and clip to the end of my days
So that nothing goes wrong. This body, this perfect body
That came from my mother's womb undiseased,
    wholesome,
No, nothing must go wrong. It is not I. It is not I.
No, it is not I. I is lodged in its head's centre,
Its turret, a little towards its eyes; it is not I, it is not I
    but it is mine
And an over-ranking shame to disease it, to let it disease.
I wash my hands, I wash my hands, I wash my hands
    once, twice, thrice,
I rinse my eyes with the sterile saline; I close, I pull the
    thick curtain,
I close the door and lock it, once, twice, thrice, I sit, I lie,
    I sleep in the great armchair,
And I sleep. Sleep, sleep is the preservative, cultivate
    sleep, it keeps me perfect.
No, no, it is not I; I lives only in the turret;
It is the body, it is the body, it is the body is the loved
    thing,
It is from my mother, it is my mother's
It came from my mother, it is an organ of the body of my
    mother
And I shall keep it with no rough touch upon it
No rough disease to ramp up and down in it. The world?
And the world? That is the mind's. In the turret. And now
    I will sleep.
I will sleep now, for my body exists. That is enough.
Something wakes me. Is it the fire?
It crackles like a speech. The buffet of winds, the cracks
Of the beams, the taste of the sun, the swimming
    shark of the moon?
No, I think, no, I think, I think I hear time flowing,
No, I think I hear time eroding, the cinder withering in the
    grate,

The Haunted Armchair

The grate withering with the time, my hands raised to my
    eyes
Where my eyes are withering, I look close at my withering
    hands. How long?
How much time have I seen withering? Did I come here
    today?
Suddenly everything grants me withering. Shall I sit here
    again?
The body is gone. I sit here alone. A nothing, a virgin
    memory.
A grease-spot. A dirty chair-back.

The Million

The number one is a good clean number;
It is like the first bold finger-stroke down a stranger's
    spine;
It is also a black obelisk with sealed doors:
On the stroke of one they open.

The number ten winks at us all
And its lids open sideways
Like certain other lips, and it is not an impossible number.

The number one hundred
Is like three people in front of a firing-squad;
Two have already fallen, collapsed.

The number one thousand is a cheap funeral
With a tricycle lugging the coffin;
The number one thousand is not large enough, even for a
    dead man.

The number ten thousand however
Begins to lean with its dark tunnel
Against its closed door;
I lean on its door to keep it shut; like an inheritance, it
    scares me.

The number one hundred thousand seems to be better
Since it immediately converts itself to a sum of money in
    a newspaper
And then to a lower figure which is the simple interest
And a very comfortable income.

The Million

But the horror of the number a million
Wipes his one long lip with her knickers
Free from the grease of the last massacred lady
Where he squats with the bones

On the glittering desert island of far greater numbers
    than he,
Circled by seas of numbers greater and more traitless
    than they.

I return to the first number, one, which is the prime candle
Muting a gracious hollow upward flame.

The Bedside Clock

I *Friend Absent*

The night is fed through the clock,
The day is fed through the clock,
It makes the day black, in columns,
The night a twitching filament,
It is a machine for making
The white black, the black brilliant.
I open the little door at the back
To watch the night go marching in its small machine,
With notched axes nodding in the dark,
And smell of armour-oil.

The world fills up with chains of little knots,
I pillow my head on heaps of quenched sparks,
Wear a shirt of ticking shadows

The night is fed through the clock,
The day is fed through the clock
In the night the stars wheel notched imagination
The day turns black with time and longing

II *Friend Present*

It sprints up silver stairs with copper heels,
It is a godown piled with ticking copper straw,
There is clock-box going on, repeated rick,
It clanks aloud in choir with each smart tick.
It is a box of crevices and gullied halls
Whose compact orchestra saws the coffined air,
Whose mainspring ebbs in glossy compressed rings,
Whose fringed wheels toss echoes deep and far
Through nimble galleries and scaffoldings,
Whose works assist each other through the steep round
    night.

The Bedside Clock

It is a clockwork pond, with bronze birds
Plumed with chinks, pecking ratchet fish. . . .
But why do I watch so curiously, and alert? Why,
I and my friend have just been going
Very deeply into the nature of things—look!
Surf of thread seethes round our skins, we draw sheets
With a whisper of blanched manes up to our chins.

The Psychologist and the Palace

There was this gong-beat that whitened the temple
    fish-ponds,
There was this great chalk-cliff that chimed the hours,
There were quiet toads with slightly blood-stained
    muzzles,
There was this orchestra of silent wind-blown torches,
And among all these marvels there was a man.

There was a pit of monsters staring at a skull,
And the monsters lay quiet for the skull had outstared
    them,
There was a good, tense silence in that pit;
There was a horse with agate hooves dancing on
    branched sparks;
There was a mechanism glittering from a blue cave-
    mouth;
There was a plaque depicting domestic effluent,
Most of it was oblong, much of it was plastic,
And the plaque made a cosiness of this fierce effluent;
There was a coral statue in a robe of bees;
And among all these marvels there was a man.

He was not to be found in the hall of candles
Where each flame had the shape of a galloping horse;
Nor by the pool where ordure floated, the size of
    bathtubs;
But I met him in the library of readers giving up writing
Whose coloured withdrawal symptoms
    muttered above their heads,
And with trembling hands took from this badly-
    frightened man
My own knapsack of heavily-sealed luck.

The Shirt, The Skull and The Grape

He pours the wine. It spins
slowly to rest. Lying still in the
spine-stemmed glass, it is his own inner head,
red, empty, unmoved.
He quaffs it down.

His shirt is now woven circuitry.
He has a computer-cuff to consult.
The cloth stirs with the life that is in it.
He has made many new friends in the colours of it.
Red darts forward with a firm handshake, blue
with its snapping eyes stands alone
on the edge of the throng, yellow giggles
uncontrollably, while green
wrapped in a mantle, sighs, and
beckons him through a vista of trees
to a monument. He sighs,
the cloth sighs. He wants
to write his experience down, and the paper stirs
with the life that is in it, and the ink sighs
and chars with enthusiasm. For a moment
he can see what he has written in black letters,
then in rending letters that swell,
then at last he glimpses his meaning
through wriggling apertures and grids
that chew themselves to ash,
dead at last.

The Shirt, The Skull and The Grape

Now he weeps, for he knows
for certain certain things he had forgotten.
He was once curator
of a particular museum skull.
It was left out of its case
in the April sun. He picked it up
to put it back and pressed
the dead bone to his cheek to feel
whether it had borrowed much warmth from the sun.
He was surprised by the vivid smell.
It came so quickly from the hole at the base of the
    cranium:
wet grass, flowing so fresh and strong
that it made a bright picture in him
for the moment that it lasted:
lush weeds growing thickly in the rain.
Each time he handled the skull
he found a fresh smell in it, smells
more complex and sustained, so he
never lacked company in the dusty little museum.
Thus he had conversations with gales and smelting
    works,
with wax, seaweed and leather,
with the stables of great racers,
with marble quarries
and the soft skins of new-born babies, among them
perhaps the baby of the skull in his hand,
with the ammonias of tragedy
and the exhilarating sweat of emperors.
It was the best friendship of his life!
He weeps, he has doubly betrayed it,
he deserted it, he forgot it.

Now he sees that the museum had a garden,
one that grew to the music of the collection.
There had been hollyhocks and honeysuckle,
three hives of bees thronging,
and in the house arrays of fine porcelain;

The Shirt, The Skull and The Grape

then for years there was thistle-music
and acrid wry nettle-sounds
and the collection of antique weapons,
halberts and spiked chain-maces;
some powerful syllable of corruption
in the black magic collection
had planted the great red agaric like sweaty beefsteak
in the fork of the strong oak there, though
a few syllables of kindness among the samplers
sprinkled persistent violets between its roots,
and the tree itself still budded green though
the strong voice that planted it was
long dead between the boards of its manuscript.
He weeps again, weeps again frankly,
he betrayed it, forgot it,
weeps, and suddenly raises his head,
looks over his shoulder through the blank wall
someone invisible is howling on the far shore

an invisible presence
hurries towards him across the water in
a line of lingering catspaws
the flowers lie flat
and spring up again as it
races into the buttercup meadow
it is the skull's person!
the pollen-dust bubble of her blows towards him
bringing vine-smells, grapes and pollen
there is a sudden shape of her
in the plaster wall
a sudden shape of her
in his back as he sits with head turned
there are gold feelings and root-smells
he brims with her
as a pitcher brims with electric current
levelling towards the wine-red brain-haunches
there is a blue flash as it touches and a shout of joy!

The Shirt, The Skull and The Grape

the deep root fits him
he is the stretched shirt of the tap-root
the vine has spread his skull like petals
roots coil from his nine apertures
from his twenty digits like wooden nails
bark-faced, bough-tongued,
ear-antlered, eye-axled,
twig-snotted, cock-shafted,
arse-beamed, branch-burst and crowned
with all the grapes ever crushed
rising terrace upon race crown upon crown of fruit
gleaming galleries and mountainous soft pastures
citrine and black cloud-wreathed pinnacles;
the sun and the
forgotten life within him
force wavering meadows of raw
grape-flowers through
the cobbled upland slopes.

For Penelope

Frankenstein in the Forest

'I am afraid for the meat
Of my illegitimate son
In the warm autumn.
When will the lightning come?'
Much wisdom had congregated there
In the open-air laboratory which is a cemetery
Under the great oaks
In the litter of acorns:
Mute parcels of impending forests.
There are grim-mouthed toads
Flocked round a boulder of quartz
Deep, complex and prodigious
That gloams in its depths
And twitches there as with a flutter of lightning.
On a portable radio
The size of a hymn-book
A harpsichord plays Scarlatti,
It suffers an attack of amnesia
As the lightning steers near.
The darkness has eaten everything except his face
The alert wise face
Backed by a view of tossing trees,
The bones of his skull
Are as loose as the leaves of the forest,
'I will send lightning through him
It will live under his skin
It will heal his mouldering
Undead bric-à-brac of other men.

Frankenstein in the Forest

There are so many bibles
Without a crack of light;
Mine has pages of slate
With fossils clearly inscribed,
Leather from racehorses
And crocodiles,
Thin frying leaves of electricity
That lies obediently in its place,
Man-skin, oak-bark and quartz. . . .'
The marble grave-stones
Are covered with equations
In the master's quick black analytick crayon,
Their stone books open at only one page;
'It is my great lightning son
Dressed in metal and bark
And the limbs of departed men,
Lightning peers out of his eyes;
He will heal their mouldering.
It is time
To raise him on the sizzling platform.'
The lightning makes a blue cave of the forest,
It strikes violently at a hawthorn tree,
A sweet smell fills the air,
It has blossomed heavily.
Now the bright blue
Thistling sparks have stuck to his poles,
His crystal machine
Fills with spangled golden oil.
His golden beehives' buzz rises to a wail
And the monster ascends on its winches,
The clouds draw up their heavy black pews
The rain falls
And the lightning services.

The storm clears.

Frankenstein in the Forest

Cloud-men are digging
Deep blue graves in the sky.
Out of the machine steps
The man, mute, complex and prodigious,
His clothes flickering with electricity,
His first murder not due until tomorrow.

Damn' Great Oaths

I *Mary*

I lay my hands on her hips as if taking an oath.
Shall I bring her nature back balanced out of these
    interesting depths?
Her hips balance; the black bible
Balances on the bedside table like an old
Friend cuckolded.
He cannot turn his skin-bound pages,
A few sun-bars rest there, tigerishly.
I lay my hands on her skin
That smoothly binds those interesting depths.
My old friend's pages are bound, and black as his boards.
Where is the brighter blackness? Where I take my oath.
I see a look grow
That becomes frightening in the pupils of her blackness,
And I give backword. Rest, rest, perturbéd book.

II *Jane*

Bread, water, and the hound's sigh of the water-closet.
Shall young babies bell at the sunlight afresh?
Or shall heat rise from the fresh-turned grave like anger?
Why is there a sunset-cloud wandering round the wood?
Why is there a puddled clay at our threshold
That looks like an indistinct fury, a last wretchedness
And a mess of broken commandments? The sky
Over-reaches all, like silk, and a clock without hands.
The park is a smouldering wick, smutty with giggles
Which gives off its birds like a guttering wickedness
And a one great wing of black thoughts, all saluting.
God loses me my balance, and recovers it for me,
    quickly.
Now maybe all hell goes into her body
Otherwise the sky is a mess of broken commandments,
And a last wretchedness, quirming with foottread,
Instead of a new young baby belling back at the sunlight.

The Half-Scissors

Humming water holds the high stars.
Meteors fall through the great fat icicles.
Spiders at rest from skinny leg-work
Lean heads forward on shaggy head-laces
All glittering from an askew moon in the sky:
One hinge snapped; a white door dislocated.
The night leans forward on this thin window;
Next door, tattered glass,
Wind twittering on jagged edges.
Doors beat like wings wishing to rise.
I lean forward to this thin fire.
A woman leaves—even the flames grow cool—
She is a one hinge snapped, I am a half-scissors.

The Mother, The Daughter and the Sighing Bridge

Great square shadows like windows sliding on the
    mountains,
pockets of cold air, travelling shivers,
ghost-pavilions.
                  Such a very
capable young man and such a
loving daughter, they must needs
at that love-age love each other.
Pocket of warm air, life-pavilion,
travelling shiver of desire
rose-tinted palanquin
silk-windowed
calling to mind our Mother the Sun
parting folded clouds to wash in light;
perfumes almost cruel, musky as legs,
pocket of warm perfumes
held by the curtains as an animal in a cage
that would tear the heart out of him
he who would part the curtains, the bridegroom
greeting her arrival in the far village.
Now the farewells, the poor
carcass of love palpitating within,
stout retainers with strong staves,
She packed in a palanquin with a passable dowry

my dear I shall visit sparingly

riders from the groom, she has not come
would you renegue on my love

The Mother, The Daughter and the Sighing Bridge

she left, as I am a woman
though an old one, and though they say
the devil walks in a dry place, I'm not
your mother-in-law devil-woman
(not yet, said a small sound inside)

Was she broken in some chasm?
there is no chasm
one road threading together two far villages
riders scoured the hills but the no traces
were so plain
no life in the mountain
just the road and sheets of stone
and great square cloud-shadows
like windows sliding open
in the stone, escarpments
webbed with narrow fast torrents

the clouds slid through the wind

it is my path now
she has travelled before me
I must go the same way
make the same journey, her mother,
I will have dusty sticks and a spry fire
to warm a cold omelette
the old woman searching
for her just-to-be-married daughter
of the rose palanquin
travelling love-pavilion

and here's an illusion
my old eyes,
cold water plunge
through rocks day-warmed
raise mist-foams in the blue twilight

The Mother, The Daughter and the Sighing Bridge

trick of the air: a pebble on the road
casts a shadow to her feet. A chest on the road
casts a shadow to her feet. A temple on the road
casts a shadow to her feet. A nun on the threshold
combing long hair, saying:

I have nothing. You are welcome.
I can give you nothing. Shelter here.
I cannot help you. Rest yourself.
I have nothing in the shrine. You may sleep.
I have nothing but myself. I welcome you.
The mother lies down and drops away to sleep.

Your daughter
lives in the god's house,
his crooked house,
he breaks his crooked back into shapes that guard her
shapes that are smallest when the sun stands highest
only travellers that walk at noon
may enter his crooked house made of shadows
they are weakest then
it is difficult to find his shadows then
belly-slithering into the secret shadows
and the guardians sleep at noon
except that within the house there is
a sleepless wicked bridge
thick and long that picks up happiness
harmony of happiness or lightness in the heart
of the belly-slithering traveller
any music or loving, it swings the bridge,
magnifies any praise in the heart
thrums to its pitch
faster and wider, catapulting your happiness
as far as the village of your birth,
flings you off to start your search again
from the utter beginning

The Mother, The Daughter and the Sighing Bridge

as a new-born. Your daughter
travelled it unconscious,
travel it unconscious, or with a conscience
of some bad deed so fresh in you
that not a joy shows

only evil creatures with evil thoughts can travel it
it is a happy creature starved of goodness
it knows happiness and wakes to it
commits an evil deed the better for once-happiness
lying under the house at the god's back.
You will have to have an evil purpose to cross it
to have done an evil thing to repass that way.
You must become evil, or never see your daughter.

She woke to light,
ear against a little stone post,
a small voice within, receding.
The shadow of the post
made a narrow trap-door on the road
she crawls, belly-slithering, shrinking.
It is a great bridge-lodge
made of towering shadows bolted to shadows
it is cool, it smells of hessian
the bridge is thick and hairy
tangled hessian, woven loosely
long-bearded and sopping with moisture
reeking of damp, mildew-streaked
unsafe! unsafe!
but she is happy!
her heart cries
Daughter! I am coming
she seizes the hairy ropes
they rock to her cry
they bristle, they swell
as bushes swell in the wind,

The Mother, The Daughter and the Sighing Bridge

like bushes, they sigh
and below
the villages of the world pass by like a foaming torrent
a torrent of pictures and people
studded with bubbles
each bubble a womb questing
through the future for its falling soul
if she should fall!
she hugs skinnily
the bridge swings her over
she hangs back downwards, face twisted over her
    shoulder
her terror quietens it

backwards she crawls into the shadow-shelter
shadow bolted to shadow
time passes, the lodge grows larger

there are bamboos growing
the only things not made of shadow
there is a shadow-table now
it has grown
shadow-goblets
and asleep in his arms
a black guardian
very small, like an infant
and infant's banqueting-furniture
they are growing
to wake with adult wrath

there are bamboos growing
she has a knife

now she has a spear

now the bridge is rock-steady
hard as masonry

The Mother, The Daughter and the Sighing Bridge

the hawsers are taut
she wishes god's death
for her human daughter

of this death she remembers
nothing

but the god turned and was ready
with his great sheaf of mandibles
a watery quiver
and she with paltry quavering fingers
lifted her dress
her important place glistened
and the god looked
bending so low
his nape was
the important place
she placed her spear
and done, she forgot it

the bridge stout as masonry, and as silent
the bearers running
the shadow palanquin rocking
spilling a little dusky perfume
she running over the bridge
that seems frozen with revulsion
detecting no happiness
in the heart of the deicide
past the great shadow-guardian
head fallen in table-litter
shadow-meat rotting about him

step out of the post's shadow
old woman, bearers and palanquin
the rose-curtains open
spilling love-musk over mother and daughter

The Mother, The Daughter and the Sighing Bridge

the two poor carcasses of love weeping and laughing
    together
she is fierce for her daughter, that old woman

thin dry grass
at the base of the post
some gossamer bridging an earth-crack
unnoticed a toe snaps it
disturbing a locust
whose shadow moves off a thin grass-stalk
impaling his shadow-nape, a silhouette
like a nun with long hair, the jaws
like a great comb turning,
this insect leaves this milestone
launches off whirring,
mother and daughter laughing
smiling and pointing
in the late sun
their magnified shadows
laughing and pointing

From Love's Journeys

from benevolent moon springs
to sharp small-apple witheredness.
I focus the moon in my
new glasses, I thought
clouds steamed from her
with the friction as she flew
but it resembles now a small
withered apple, and the sky
is hung with stars like
small bright
wrinkling apples, the autumn
is hung full with them, the fruit
has been too long upon
the tree, small withered apples
are the sweetest, gather them up.

VII

A fat confluent
sparrow alights
adjusting the tension
of the whole tree's twigs,
he pipes high I AM
THE CHAIRMAN OF THE LABURNUM COMMITTEE
as the raving pollen beneath his claws
zips loose in soft masses.

VIII

My biologist friend
had many accomplishments, he would
incubate a snake's egg, or the
egg of one of the great fishes
within a test-tube packed
in a great straw box and then
dissect out the small curled
squab or embryo setting it
in its jelly into a special
ring with a small hinged

door and placing this
on his earfinger would
prod said finger into
his head and listen
to the unborn wisdom of
the unconscious snake,
the wide-eyed unliving fish.
He had hair that was
tangled and scurfy, you
could work a radio on so much detail,
and he certainly picked up
useful sayings, such as
you must keep your Teresa alight.

IX

I was travelling in a
cloud of antique
musical instruments when
she threw her
catafalque at me. The
crowd started to cheer, then
fell silent like the wall
of bricks that faces
a firing squad. Afterwards they
started laughing again and
could not be stopped. Fog-signals
bombed distantly. I waited
for the locked
carriage-load of virgins to be
pushed off the dock. The air
curdled as it rolled
forward, a yellow mire
of shrill voices
spilled from its
interior, I realised that
its lamps were not filled

From Love's Journeys

with light only, but
were also packed with the
tortured-filament's terror,
visible screaming. I watched
the foliated equipage
part the waters, I saw
the waters heal their
oily rainbow again, and I saw
that her dress
was of that self-same
yellow that
screamed as she moved.

I immediately rose
and swiftly
shaved myself free of that dream.

X

Love unites
shock
and permanence
and drink
is a combination
of idiocy
and celibacy, or
so I reflect
crouched at a table
in a Western Region buffet bar
with the sunlight
sliding rapidly through
the train's windows
like notes on a mouthorgan,
like country tunes.

XI

She offered him a blue
thistle-flower, parting the

semen-soft head he found that she
had tucked a white
aspirin into the blue
flock. He pondered
the meaning of her gesture:
she was the anodyne
among the blue sheets; his seed
contained an
anodyne for her
aches; he needed
an anodyne for his
mentality which was too
intrusive was it during
intuitive blue intercourse; his
sex needed an aspirin
to stop the nagging; and he
mentioned the matter to
the other woman who said it
was simple: drugs
including drink were of
too excremental a
whiteness.

XII

I did not wish her
to erase the night
not at first but
she sliced such
great holes in beautifully: I
was only inquiring, and we sleep
late into the morning. Instead
of night I have
the blue flash
of a nylon shirt stripped off in the darkness
the sudden

crackle after sleep of radio static
on a blank waveband at morning's four o'clock.

XIII

He is at ease in mud. He
folds it around him
like a great dark
cloak, this is because
he lives in a house
of mischievous children, they have
dim idle hands in the
twilit rooms, he
rebukes them sharply, they weep
tears like rotting icicles, and she
wears a nitrocotton nightdress, she
is sheathed in potential explosions.
But the mud is soft and dark, and will
not, whatever you do to it,
explode, and ablutions
after it are a gross
rewarding priestlike task,
under the lustrous garden hose
enclosed in the starlit glitter.

XIV

When I woke up
I was in bed
with my boots on, and
my wife was nowhere to
be found, I had not
convinced myself
even now of
the innocence and
purity of
her cavities which
I had caused to be
sealed by the

From Love's Journeys

introduction of
contraceptive
devices, so, as I
thought, she would
have leisure to rub
mint into my
beard so that
every thread felt
green and I would have
big eyes like
hanging mirrors and in
each hair of my head
would ramp innumerable
golden lions.

XV

Let us
have all our
divorce-courts floored
in hardish lard, so that
the emotional heat
of her lawyer's plea
sinks him
until he is stifled.
Encourage in these
places cool advocates
with cool heads
and cool limbs signifying
combustible hearts.

XVI

If god had intended
us to run on
all fours he
would have made us
cowards. I wanted a
boat constructed so that

it would melt
in the middle of
the pond: *I wanted
to save the lady.* But she
was not bothered, she had
a tongue like a hot
snail and even her
wristwatch was
carnal: I took it
to the jeweller and he
mended it like a man
picking meat from
a lobster-claw.

XVII
There's nothing
so dead
as an old
hymn-book. The cathedral
is built like
a hollow spinal-column,
the crown of the
head to the east, the marrow
missing. If it were
filled with a sparkling
electrical jelly, star-
jelly, it would be evident
that proper
worship was
from outside, on
the cathedral lawns. As it is
people leave from the
apertures like running
nostrils. Let
fish swim as fish, peach
settle into peach, the
goldfish
below, the peaches

glowing
on the boughs above, the
clouds scudding in
the water and the
church
electrical.

XVIII

Oh yes. Fascinating. I've
never been so
insulted in my life. It was
quite charming. And in that
hat too. Of course
the Hat is the Mother. Except
when you turn it
inside out. Then
it's the Father. He gave me
porridge. I've never been
so fascinated. Or was it
insulted? Porridge of course symbolises
the Holy Ghost. That is
when the Holy Ghost is
lying down. When the
porridge flies, then
that's the time to
look out. And of course
flies are a symbol of
the female genitals.
Oh yes. Except when they
buzz. She put
her false mandible in
upside down. I know
what that meant, of
course. But you must
keep that
under your Hat. I've
never been so
fascinated.

From Love's Journeys

XX

A great forked tongue
of light licked up
the people streaming into
the Big Top where the
Duchess of Cunt was waiting
to award me my
school prize of sex-
instruction booklets, her
admonishing voice boomed
distantly in the forking
quagmires of my brain
and for the first time
even the headmaster
looked forked under the
black curtain he wore. And
Her Grace's face was
twisted to the left and
beautifully powdered and looked
like a carefully-laundered
sheet badly-ironed waving on
a forked flagstaff.

XXI

Pebbles in the wood, people
in the wood, sheep-skulls
in the wood, all
listen to the small rigid
radio-sets the size of
psalters full of
gay laughter, is there any
difference between the full
and empty darkness?

XXII

How well policed the
sky is tonight with

rapid squads, we
shall have rain to
forgive us in the morning.

XXIII

A car moving across the rim of the far cliff like a gleaming mineral particle detached from the strata.

The cliff below me like a great cannon shooting at the clouds with the sea.

Below, a white rose swirling in the foam between the rocks; it runs with brilliant white legs up the stones.

There are big lichened boulders lying sunk in the upland meadows like rugous starfish awaiting the return of the sea.

Then rain comes dashing over the sea like the prow of an immense white ship made of glimmer and mist. It comes straight at me and I am peppered with harmless bullets.

After that I felt real in the landscape, the grass settled into grass, the birds moved black as pips in a rectangular pattern in the sky, like a high figure of dots on a blue dice fortunately-fallen. My skin and my eyeskin had been rinsed open by the rain. I felt as though I had been caught up in a whirlwind, and let down again gently, my skin glowing and my hair wet.

The little shabby teahouse was a haven from a lot, though the immense clouds moving rapidly outside were not enemies. They shook gently across the uncurtained window like curds across a blue stone tablet, the soft agreeable to the hard.

XXIV

My nerves jump as she
grins at me, but
there is a better
picture of her in my
head. I lose possession of

myself sometimes between her
legs but then she
often gives me back
myself manifold in a body
that feels blue and grey; in
the black and white that still
hovers when she grins
I am nowhere.

XXV

The baby sees all. Giants
stride with giant pores,
they hiccup
thunderously. She falls
into mother's nostrils
like a cathedral through which
a tobacco-stained breeze
flows. Father's voice
arrives like blue-black
thunders, she responds
with sounds like
green apricots.

XXIX

The medusa thought so
hard of the plight of
humanity that snakes sprang from
the head she scratched so hard. When men
looked at her they changed into art, because
she was such a
beauty that she moved
through them like a
tune that was so slow and
grand they turned to
stone. This was not her
purpose at
all. She made marble with

too much conceiving, and the snakes were the
unbent and free-coiling convolutions before
packed and frozen within the stone
head-hutch of this great
woman.

XXX

He had been
turned to stone
from the waist down. He
thought how
lucky the sundial was
absorbed in its time-
telling. His body bled
at the seam, was laved and
bound in a surgical
cummerbund. His
genitals were entire
though chipped because he
had fallen in
love with a
granite foreshore. The stone
seeds in him had yearned, but
his soft parts above the
waist would not believe and lost
him in fantasy as his stone
loins strove and clinked in
week-long ecstasies.

XXXI

The summer air outside was
striped with shadows of
grass and trees, we had opened the
window and the tiger stepped over
the sill on to the striped carpet like
suddenly-moving striped air. I had observed
such intrusions before in a spider that

moved fast like crooked shadows or a
universal small crack in things
always running somewhere. Now
we had the tiger and outside the
trees moved in soft
small gestures like a baby's
hands.

XXXII

She washed the waters with
her beauties, white; all the
world's waters were the
better for her baths, her
bathroom was a powerhouse of
cleaner waters rippling
down her plughole through the
purer sewers into the
purer sea, had she lived
long enough the sea would have been
clean at last and the stars
would come down to
bathe, and every time she
pulled her
lavatory chain new
rifts of ore went shining down.

XXXIII

Family bible:
stout leather bottle
containing a speckled
white fluid.
Mother insists
the black
bits
are nourishing: I see her still
reading hers
at the kitchen table

grasping a knife
slicing pearly onions
and weeping freely
at the story of how rousingly nourishing
Jezebel was to the palace dogs.

XXXV

Our president rots
in his bedroom, hélas.
It is a once-bright
country. It was. The flags have been
at half-mast for
generations, the wigs
of the
flunkeys are their own
fallen hair. The wombs
are full of
blank faces and blood. Only
underground, far beneath
the exhausted soil the
great rocks still
wing silently.

XXXVI

My father advised me
to lose no time
in drawing in my
horns
leaning back in
his soft leather chair and
clothing his head
from his cigar
with a
beautiful seamless billowing
shirt of grey
silk that immediately
began to rend itself.

Dr Faust's Sea-Spiral Spirit

I am frightened. It makes velvet feel too tall.
Its crest peers in at the library window and I cannot open
    the books,
They hug themselves shut like limpets months after it has
    gone.
The roses have learnt to thunder,
They spread petals like peals of red thunder echoing,
The sky looks like blue boxes of white powder being
    smashed by grey fists.
God is an angel in an angel, and a stone in a stone,
But everything enters this, and is gone.
That cry makes everything look afraid
And how small a whisper do we hear of him
Merely the brushing of his outer garment.

It passes pallidly over the meadow
And suddenly it is brilliant with pollen
It will now seek out female fields of flowers
It cannot help that, they will draw him.
It will pass through a field of bulls
And every hair will be stripped
And every bone broken
But the seed will spin on
A column of translucent horn pulled to the cows
Its seething tip.
It will so use a city
For the sake of one woman.

It destroyed an archipelago.
It was selecting human organs and a dhoti.
It reverses direction and is a person

Dr Faust's Sea-Spiral Spirit

For I have spoken to him, and he inhales deeply
And thinks deeply, and he speaks and he ceases speaking
Then there is an unforgettable perfume on the air
The woman to fit which I will seek for ever,
And an unforgettable tune for her to walk to.

That cry makes everything look afraid.
The bones float up to the ceiling and the iron bar bends.
It strips a whale for its immense bones
And stands the empty meat on its tail.
The rapid alteration of perfumes in it
Will kill with alternation of memories.
It is a shop of carpets furling and unfurling.
The plain pinafores alert themselves
And are a hive of angry spots.
It is a house of wineglasses and towering butter and
    cabbages
And its scream is the cry of wool under torment
Or a silk scream, and it is constructed like buttons
And I cannot hear what he is saying
For the wool-and-bone
Screaming at me of his buttons.
Yet the practised shaman
Drums until it appears,
Runs up its sides and travels the whole earth over,
Pees over its crown, a magical act
It is his glass ladder to heaven, his magical cannon
That can be fired once only, what nonsense!
Master Alice descended it, inspecting the good things
Arrayed on its shelves, it may also be summoned
By wounding the air upwards
With a rifle, or by burning Dresden
(There it was seen spinning between
Ranks of buildings gustily burning,
Casting light from winged chevrons), or
By laying the Tarot in an anti-clockwise pattern.

Dr Faust's Sea-Spiral Spirit

I suspect it and its wife are responsible for Moses' head
And the ten great transmissions whose echoes never stop
Piped along the pair of them hurt my head too
Among all the others.
It will also let down as on a four-cornered cloth
Ancient gifts and treasures, such as
A whole slum of Ambergris like a
Giant's pock-marked skull in curly earwax.

God was found with his head poxed to the bone
He had walked through a hungry cloud of it
It is everywhere it is one and many
It is ships of the desert-seas that sail fleets of it
It stands in linked chains on a calm among icebergs
It is playing its enormous chess and takes a berg with
    one of itself
Crashing a boom, and it takes each other
With a twang like a bridge breaking,
At Christmas dinner I have cracked it
Out of the brown dust of a walnut and as the bathwater
    runs out
It tickles my toes, it is manifold behind the iron doors
Of the neglected casemate, swinging
And breathing in restless thickets,
They say space is sewn of it and I have seen it pouring
    through the telescope
There it is at the north pole shining with the moon
And with the midnight sun, go to the south pole you will
    find it there too,
And between them they keep us all spinning
Growing so tall their crests freeze and throw off
Ice-circlets sparkling, flying diadem upon diadem
Called UFO by the observers, scrutinizing our latitudes.
And yet I have known it
Stand still at my right hand long enough
I have opened the little cupboard in its flank
And plucked out the small brown monkey who lives there
Who became my friend and stayed with me a good while.

It wrenched itself from the head, and the head listened
    with its lack,
It wrenched itself from the rock, and the snail crept in its
    wake.
To Red Indians it always carries a dead spider gently in
    its buzzing jaws
As the refugee mother carries her dead baby many miles
    in the dusk.
The anatomist tells me I have a pair of small idols of it set
    in my head
That are the kernel of hearing: the tone-deaf apparition
Is a river on tiptoe, rhythmically digesting its own bed.
But it is also a band of eyes and a solid wall of God
Seeking embrace, and it is the great one from the North
That opens like theatre-curtains and there are four beasts
    marching
With a man on a throne inside, but I know too
That it sets with a click and leaves skimming on the
    waves
The great pearly nautilus that lets out its sails and scuds
    gently off
Its inhabitant glowing dimly through the thin shell walls
A coil of luminous foam by night and a swimming red
    bone by day.
Thus it seems to me. To itself
It is trees, with high leafy galleries
And scrolls of steel, equation-shaped; a man, bearded,
Strolls up its staircase, a bird
Alights on its branches. With our spiral stairs
We have built it homage, it mounts itself in homage
To its own perfected double helix; that crucifix
Dangling between your breasts is a long-section of it.

Like the unicorn's horn it is male and female at once
And emits waves of all lengths from intense internal
    friction,
It will make a white sound on your transistor
Though a few notes of church organ might fly together:

Dr Faust's Sea-Spiral Spirit

Chance will have it so among all the other sounds;
And the electricity that branches through its lacquered
    walls
Is of a purer fine than armature-power, that whining sham;
You can time a great clock on its global pulse.
It is the pouring tower of pebbles
That walks the coast glittering in the cool evening,
It is trees among trees that are trees
Until it decides to leave the forest by revolution.

But men have pinned the giant down in clocks and
    churches
I watch its face wounded hour after hour
Behind the glass of my bedside clock,
Hacked into numbers, plucked
By enumerating metal
Welded inside a castle:
Within its fortress-windows rounded axes
Powered by its replica in metal
Chink like milled money
Fiscal time
But I would love to go to the church
And be served by its priest
In whirling petticoats
Where the Host
Greasy with electricities
Flies into our mouths
Like flocks of roasted pigeons.
It changes places
With Job continually.
It carries seven directions in itself
And five elements,
Music, and thunder,
And small gods laughing with patient happiness.

Slice it low down and find a fish
Lower still, granite and chrysoprase
Fairly high, the embryo babe in water

Dr Faust's Sea-Spiral Spirit

Higher still, his wail winds out of the wound
He travels at youth-speeds
In the slimmer reaches
Moves zodiac-slow with beards
Through the greater girths.
I take a sip
From the cup chained to its waist.
Faust shunted himself.
Indeed he tamed it
Peered through the sea in it
Inspected the mountain for gems.
I saw him bounding over the Carpathians
Like a child on a pogo-stick.
To cheat the devil he was interred in it four hundred
    years.
Its grip over the land has eased.
Warm summer breezes
Flow from its palm
Faust strolls happily
Through its flowering palms.
At the bow, the atom; at the stern, the zodiac.

The atomic bomb is a bad picture of it, clumsy and
    without versatility,
It discriminates not at all, and there are too many bad
    things to say about it,
I will not spend time on that figment of the thing I am
    talking about.
It hums like a top and its voice smashes volcanoes,
Yet it will burrow and from the riflings of Etna
Speed skyward, hurtling pillar of red rock.
The mouth is not necessarily a one-way trip
Though you should take plenty of room.
It has shaggy lips, a necklace of pines.
It electrifies Perranporth sand-dunes
Every grain crackles and hums
In flickering organ-notes under
My blue slippered prints.

Dr Faust's Sea-Spiral Spirit

It is a great traveller and sometimes slips
Up its own back-passage to assuage its terrible wander
    lusts.
When men and women embrace
They impersonate it
They are a cone of power
An unbuilt beehive
We two are a brace of them behaving as one
We invaginate, evaginate,
Time stops inside us.

In it the ticking
Of innumerable stolen clocks
Welds to an organ-note.

It is sometimes made of lightning
And at others nothing but magnetism.
It is a kind of knot
Too intricate to undo
Too virile to pull tight.
Untied, a world explodes,
Tied, it winks out.
Or it hovers
Too restless
To untie the human knot.
It is the last trumpet
And the first trumpet.
It fashioned Glastonbury Tor
With helical fingermarks.
The burglar by night bears
Ten small tough patterns of it
Through the polished house,
Each one speaks his name.
It is a kind of walking cliff
And a walking well.
The fossil shell and the empty penis
Alike await this wakener.
The Master comes!

Dr Faust's Sea-Spiral Spirit

He shuts his blue snuff-box
And the wind stops.
He knows how to wind it
With a certain key
That makes the whole home disappear
Inside-out up the chimney;
Knee-deep knee-deep beware
Croaks the frog far inside it.
Its vomited bees float
Coiling down the hillside.
It has much in common
With the round-dance and cyclotron;
It will hover
Over the winding dance on the sand-beach
It will suddenly reverse
The people vanish and all that is left is a shell.
The Master says, learn from this power,
It is strapped to your wrist like an oyster
And allow it to descend into your mouth
And suck you dry
And let it pluck out your eyes
So they can ride on the storm.
Is the shaft weary?
If this shaft is not tired
There is no tiredness anywhere;
If this shaft is tired
Wait for the new world.
Subdue it if you dare.
My master did.
The long thin one enters
The open lid of his cranium,
Screws down his spine,
Sets with a click.
My master wakes,
Gets up and laughs suddenly,
Totters widdershins picking things up
Favouring his left hand
Since this is the northern hemisphere.

Dr Faust's Sea-Spiral Spirit

And it whirls directly over his head—
Do not look up, it is his hypnotist!
And the sun, that squints through its sun-spots.

It is the best of rainstorms
Since it so mightily collects
And so mightily lets fall.
It has subdued the great sea-worm
Who hangs upright, frothing in its embrace.
Throw a knife into it
You will wound the heel of a grey witch
Who will not bleed, she is made of cobwebs.
It is the spirit of the sealed boulder
It was born of a beach-pebble, and left by a pock,
It is the spirit of the oil-gusher, the black that yellow
    burns.
It touches the rock, that rock
Speeds up and is petrol for motor-cars:
A spark of its friction catches
The rock is no more in a shuddering flap! But mostly
It buries this rock-spirit until it is needed.
I will call it a magical name in the Linnean system
Vortex macromphalos and I carry on my watchchain
A silky cocoon reminding me of its quiet moments
Of its transformation and presence anywhere:
In the gnat-swarm with smoky feet,
Faltering in spirals; in the tons
Of aching black-water-muscle poised over the campus
Peering in through the long library-windows;
In four winds bound round in one breast and breeze.

Dr Faust's receipt for THE NAILS
    Seek out its unfreighted apparition
    It will be a shimmer between oaks at evening
    Celebrated glancingly by gnats
    In broken spirals, falling and rising.
    Anoint with the lizard. It will turn horn-white.
    Now take nails of sweet-tasting iron
    Drive your nails into the floating bone
    Strike it as it returns each time
    Draw sparks with your blows, keep it
    Spinning, persist. The Whirlwind
    Will shrink, measuring gradually
    Its substance into the nail
    That falls to the grass heavily.
    You may use this nail for many benefits.
    Drive it into rock and the hill will be glass,
    You may peruse its secrets.
    Drive it into a table of dry wood
    It will bloom like a bridefeast.
    Drive it into the skull of a blind man
    He will see men like trees walking.

                    For Julie Kendrick